SEPTEMBER 2018

Sunday	Monday	Tuesday	Wednesday	Thursday	Friday	Saturday
						1
2	3 Labor Day	4	5	6	7	8
9 Rosh Hashanah begins at sundown Grandparents Day	10 Islamic New Year begins at sundown	11	12	13	14	15
16	17	18 Yom Kippur begins at sundown	19	20	21 International Day of Peace	22
23 / 30	24 Queen's Birthday (WA Australia)	25	26	27	28	29

OCTOBER 2018

Sunday	Monday	Tuesday	Wednesday	Thursday	Friday	Saturday
	1 Labour Day (ACT, NSW & SA Australia) Queen's Birthday (QLD Australia)	2	3	4	5	6
7	8 Columbus Day Observed Thanksgiving (Canada)	9	10	11	12 Traditional Columbus Day	13
14	15	16	17	18	19	20
21	22 Labour Day (New Zealand)	23	24	25	26	27
28	29	30	31 Halloween			

NOVEMBER 2018

Sunday	Monday	Tuesday	Wednesday	Thursday	Friday	Saturday
				1	2	3
4 U.S. Daylight Saving Time ends at 2:00 a.m.	5	6 Election Day	7	8	9	10
11 Veterans Day Remembrance Day (Canada)	12	13	14	15	16	17
18	19 Mawlid an-Nabi begins at sundown	20	21	22 Thanksgiving	23	24
25	26	27	28	29	30	

DECEMBER 2018

Sunday	Monday	Tuesday	Wednesday	Thursday	Friday	Saturday
						1
2 Hanukkah begins at sundown	3	4	5	6	7	8
9	10	11	12	13	14	15
16	17	18	19	20	21	22
23 / 30	24 / 31	25 Christmas	26 Kwanzaa Boxing Day	27	28	29

JANUARY

2019

Sunday	Monday	Tuesday	Wednesday	Thursday	Friday	Saturday
"Let's be merry; we'll have tea and toast . . . and an endless host of syllabubs and jellies and mince pies." —PERCY BYSSHE SHELLEY		1 NEW YEAR'S DAY	2 BANK HOLIDAY (SCOTLAND & NEW ZEALAND)	3	4	5
6	7	8	9	10	11	12
13	14	15 MARTIN LUTHER KING JR.'S BIRTHDAY	16	17	18	19
20	21 MARTIN LUTHER KING DAY	22	23	24	25	26 AUSTRALIA DAY (AUSTRALIA)
27	28	29	30	31		

THE TEAPOT

A NEW YEAR'S DAY GATHERING

With a whole new year to look forward to, gather friends around a festive tea table and share "the cup that cheers." A pretty cake, enrobed in icing as white as new-fallen snow, tempts each arriving guest from atop its gilded stand. Who will cut the first slice? In England in times past, it was considered good luck if the cutter of the cake was a dark-haired woman. And to ensure future good fortune in the household, every guest had to have a taste. This charming "Gold Swirl" teapot was produced in the 1920s by James Sadler & Sons, Ltd., of Stoke-on-Trent, England. Founded in 1882, the pottery was initially famous for its sturdy earthenware Brown Betty teapots. But after a 1928 visit to America by Edward Sadler, the firm began to make clever novelty teapots of very high quality. Among the most famous were a series of old-fashioned "Crinoline Ladies" teapots and a dashing Art Deco racing car pot with the tea-themed license plate OK T 42.

TEA ACCESSORIES

THE ELEGANT SPOON TRAY

Starting in the 1690s, when teacups were not yet accompanied by saucers, it was customary for prosperous tea drinkers to have a special receptacle on the table for spoons. The small oblong trays, around 6½ inches long and 4 inches wide, and known as spoon trays, solved the problem of where to rest one's teaspoon when it was not in use. Made of china or silver, the trays were often part of tea sets made by Worcester and Caughley.

FEBRUARY

2019

Sunday	Monday	Tuesday	Wednesday	Thursday	Friday	Saturday
"Oh, Valentine! You could be My cup of tea!" —Motto from a vintage valentine					1	2
3	4	5 Lunar New Year	6 Waitangi Day (New Zealand)	7	8	9
10	11	12 Lincoln's Birthday	13	14 Valentine's Day	15	16
17	18 Presidents Day	19	20	21	22 Washington's Birthday	23
24	25	26	27	28		

THE TEAPOT

A PERFECTLY LOVELY TEA

Pink-theme tea parties, especially ones held on Valentine's Day, were in vogue in the late 1800s. Cookbooks and periodicals provided hostesses with detailed instructions on everything from choosing the correct centerpiece (preferably of tinted spun sugar) to softly illuminating the table with pink Fairy Lamps. Most delightful of all would have been a table adorned with this exquisite Royal Worcester tea set. Specially made in England in 1893 for a Boston department store, it has a pink edge wash and a dainty raised shot enamel trim. Frequent tea-party attendees were well informed about all of the popular tea-drinking superstitions. Not wanting to jinx the path to love and marriage, they knew to spoon the sugar into their tea before adding milk. And they were thrilled to find undissolved sugar in the bottom of their empty teacup—it meant that someone was sweet on them.

THE TEA TABLE

ROMANTIC FAIRY LAMPS

In 1857, London-based candle manufacturer Samuel Clarke patented the Fairy Lamp, a decorative domed-glass shade covering a chubby candle set in a glass cup. First used as a nightlight, the lamps, which gave off a soft, radiant glow, were soon made in a variety of shapes, designs, and colors. This elaborate Fairy Lamp epergne has three prunus-patterned Queen's Burmese lamps on crystal arms, an elevated matching bowl for fruit or flowers, and graceful crystal fronds, all positioned on a mirrored plateau.

MARCH

2019

Sunday	Monday	Tuesday	Wednesday	Thursday	Friday	Saturday
"Teatime provided a quiet little hour for refinement and gossip." —Virginia T. Elverson and Mary Ann McLanahan, *A Cooking Legacy*, 1975					1	2
3	4 Labour Day (WA Australia)	5	6 Ash Wednesday	7	8	9
10 U.S. Daylight Saving Time begins at 2:00 a.m.	11 Labour Day (VIC Australia)	12	13	14	15	16
17 St. Patrick's Day	18	19	20	21	22	23
24 / 31	25	26	27	28	29	30

THE TEAPOT

IT'S ALWAYS TIME FOR TEA

Given life's ceaseless hurly-burly, it's no small comfort to know that it's always time for tea. In the snug intimacy of the tea table, worries subside, good news is celebrated, and a few snippets of harmless gossip can be shared. Life looks up after fragrant cups of tea have been dispensed from a lovely pot such as this Ridgway London-shape porcelain teapot. Made in 1810, it features a wide blue ground band decorated in what is known as a "loose" Gaudy Welsh style with touches of gold lustre. The Ridgway family were important and prolific producers of attractive high-quality earthenware and porcelain. Job Ridgway founded his Staffordshire-based Cauldon Place Works in 1802. His sons John (who would later specialize in tea wares and was appointed official potter to Queen Victoria) and William joined their father in 1808.

TEA ACCESSORIES

SILVER TEA-SPOUT STRAINERS

The ingenious tea-spout or spout strainer, one of the rarest and most costly teatime accoutrements, first appeared on elegant tea tables in the early 1800s. A small free-swinging bucket or basket with decoratively pierced holes in the bottom was attached by its handle to a pair of thin silver prongs. The prongs were inserted into the pot's spout, leaving the basket suspended. Once the pot was tilted for pouring, the strainer swung into position beneath the spout, ready to capture errant leaves before they fell into the cup.

APRIL

2019

Sunday	Monday	Tuesday	Wednesday	Thursday	Friday	Saturday
	1	2 Lailat al Miraj begins at sundown	3	4	5	6
7	8	9	10	11	12	13
14 Palm Sunday	15	16	17	18	19 Good Friday Passover begins at sundown	20
21 Easter	22 Earth Day Easter Monday Bank Holiday (Eng., Wales, N. Ire., Austral., N.Z.)	23	24	25 Anzac Day (Australia & New Zealand)	26	27
28	29	30				

"Where words cease, music begins, and where music ceases, kissing begins."

—Norman Douglas

THE TEAPOT

TEA IN THE CONSERVATORY

The neoclassical lines of this Wedgwood Jasperware echo the lyrical pleasures of teatime in the conservatory. What Mozart is to music, Josiah Wedgwood (1730–1795) is to teapots. Known as "the potter to the world," he asked his wife to try out each new teapot to ensure its usefulness. He conducted nearly 4,000 experiments before perfecting the stoneware he called Jasperware. Each piece was embellished with a cameo-like, hand-applied white bas relief depicting a Greek or Roman theme. First mentioned in Wedgwood's catalog in 1787, the design was produced in a range of colors including celery green, pink, yellow, and lilac. But the elegant pale blue glaze of the first designs—a color that came to be called "Wedgwood blue"—is the best known.

TEATIME TUNES

THE SOUND OF MUSIC

The harmonious sounds of teatime—the gentle tinkling of dainty silver teaspoons against china cups, the murmurs of gossip, and the sighs of contentment accompanying the first sip of fragrant tea—all of these have inspired countless musical odes. The intimacy of a tête-à-tête is celebrated in "Tea for Two" and "When I Take My Sugar to Tea." "She Serves a Nice Cup of Tea" is praise any hostess would be grateful to receive, whether serving "Tea on the Terrace" or "Tea in Chicago." In the end, regardless of the tempo, when it comes to the matters of the heart, "Everything Stops for Tea."

YOUNG
to their
DANCE
BEECHWOOD HOUSE.

MAY

2019

Sunday	Monday	Tuesday	Wednesday	Thursday	Friday	Saturday
"Shout hurray for the flowers of May, pretty springtime flowers!" —Jean Warren			1	2	3	4
5 Ramadan begins at sundown	6 Bank Holiday (United Kingdom) Labour Day (QLD Australia)	7	8	9	10	11
12 Mother's Day	13	14	15	16	17	18
19	20 Victoria Day (Canada)	21	22	23	24	25
26	27 Memorial Day Observed Spring Bank Holiday (United Kingdom)	28	29	30 Traditional Memorial Day	31	

THE TEAPOT

THE TEA DANCE

Although the tea dance was a popular diversion from 1900 until the outbreak of World War II, its heyday was the free-spirited 1920s and 1930s. Elegantly garbed tea dance habitués eagerly gathered at five o'clock in the palm courts of fine hotels and fashionable department stores to take tea and glide fluidly across the floor to string orchestras' suave waltzes, frisky foxtrots, and lively Charlestons. The era's daring and exuberance are epitomized by the bold Art Deco-inspired designs of Clarice Cliff, produced by the Newport Pottery in Stoke-on-Trent. "Color and plenty of it" was Cliff's unofficial motto. This rare Bizarre Ware "Early Morning" set in the "Carpet" pattern, made in 1930 and 1931, included a revolutionary flat-sided "Stamford" shape teapot.

TEATIME HISTORY

TANGO TEAS

Initially called *thé dansant* in Paris, where the tango was first introduced from Buenos Aires, tango teas became the rage in fashionable London circles around 1912 and throughout Europe by 1915. More daring than the later tea dances, these sensual soirées were just naughty enough to be slightly controversial, and therefore tempting, but not sufficiently off-limits to be taboo. Attendance at some tango teas was by subscription only, and there were even tango clubs at theaters and restaurants.

JUNE

2019

Sunday	Monday	Tuesday	Wednesday	Thursday	Friday	Saturday
"Tea gives life new charm." —VINTAGE TEA ADVERTISEMENT						1
2	3 Queen's Birthday (New Zealand)	4 Eid al-Fitr begins at sundown	5	6	7	8
9	10 Queen's Birthday (Australia exc. QLD & WA)	11	12	13	14 Flag Day	15
16 Father's Day	17	18	19	20	21	22
23 / 30	24 St. Jean Baptiste Day (Canada)	25	26	27	28	29

THE TEAPOT

TEA WITH FRIENDS

There is no cozier, sweeter teatime than that shared with dear friends. The musical clink of favorite teacups and the gentle murmur of shared confidences create a soothing haven of tranquility and intimacy that nurtures the senses. Like the joy of a friendship that never fades, the fresh beauty of Royal Winton Chintz Ware is everlasting. The firm made its first chintz design at the Grimwades pottery at Stoke-on-Trent, England, in 1928. It was a teapot in a pattern called Marguerite, the design of which was inspired by an Indian chintz fabric pillow that belonged to owner Leonard Grimwade's wife. Royal Winton's dense floral patterns continued to capture the cheerful clutter of English cottage gardens. The vibrant "Welbeck" pattern teapot here, ca. 1934, features a profusion of roses, daffodils, white narcissi, tulips, and wisteria. Prized by collectors, this design was inspired by chintz fabric from Liberty of London.

THE TEA TABLE

THE LANGUAGE OF FLOWERS

Fragrant posies have long been the decorative grace note of the tea table. But during the Victorian era, they took on special significance. Every flower in the bouquet sent in thanks to a gracious hostess or to woo an adored one had a very particular meaning. The sentiments conveyed by the blossoms were codified in special manuals on the language of flowers. Red tulips were a declaration of love, and pansies said simply, "Thinking of you."

JULY

2019

Sunday	Monday	Tuesday	Wednesday	Thursday	Friday	Saturday
	1 Canada Day (Canada)	2	3	4 Independence Day	5	6
7	8	9	10	11	12	13
14	15	16	17	18	19	20
21	22	23	24	25	26	27
28	29	30	31			

". . . our excellent home made bread & fresh butter & above all the refreshment of a good cup of tea!"

—Anna McNeill Whistler

THE TEAPOT

TEA WITH WHISTLER'S MOTHER

In the early 1860s, about the time his mother, Anna, left America to join him in London, the artist James McNeill Whistler began collecting blue-and-white Oriental porcelain. Early examples first reached Europe in the 1600s on Dutch ships. From 1736 to 1795, vast quantities were made in Canton and Nanking specifically for export and were sent by sea to England along with chests of tea. This late eighteenth-century Nanking teapot with a Blue Willow-like design and an unusual double-loop handle is a typical export design. Whistler entertained lavishly, using his china, and some pieces even appeared in his paintings. In 1879, eight years after completing the famous *Arrangement in Grey and Black No. 1* portrait of his mother, the bankrupt Whistler lost his precious porcelain. Today, four of his beloved teapots are on view at the University of Glasgow's Hunterian Art Gallery.

TEAPOT HISTORY

A VERY "COSY" TEAPOT

Even expensive teapots can drip maddeningly. In 1922, Abram Allware Ltd., of Bristol, England, eliminated the spout, added a built-in strainer, and patented the dripless "Cosy" Pot in 26 countries. Made by Pountney & Co., Ltd., and Woods & Sons, coveted examples included this Yuan pattern, ca. 1929, and a rare "Seed Poppy" design ca.1923, painted by Charlotte Rhead.

AUGUST

2019

Sunday	Monday	Tuesday	Wednesday	Thursday	Friday	Saturday
"Teatime is at the well-known ebb of the afternoon." —Joan Parry Dutton, *Good Fare and Cheer of Old England*				1	2	3
4	5 Civic Holiday (Canada) Summer Bank Holiday (Scotland)	6	7	8	9	10
11 Eid al-Adha begins at sundown	12	13	14	15	16	17
18	19	20	21	22	23	24
25	26 Summer Bank Holiday (Eng., Wales, N. Ire.)	27	28	29	30	31 Islamic New Year begins at sundown

THE TEAPOT

A SUMMER SHOWER

Wedding showers call for lush floral arrangements that hint at the gorgeous bouquets sure to glorify the big event so near in the future. Fragrant tea accompanied by dainty sandwiches and bite-size, flower-garnished cakes make for the loveliest summer celebration. Is there a more appropriate teapot for the occasion than this one of hard-paste porcelain Meissen, made in 1870? The delicate beauty of its scattered relief-work flowers rivals those in nature. Ninth-century Chinese potters perfected the art of making translucent white hard-paste porcelain with a smooth glassy finish, but kept the formula a secret. In 1708, German alchemist Johann Friedrich Bottger created a similar formula after discovering kaolin, a local white clay, in Saxony. Two years later, his patron, Augustus the Strong of Saxony, a collector of Chinese and Japanese porcelain, established the first western porcelain factory at Albrechtsburg Castle in Meissen.

THE TEACUP

THE OTHER SIDE OF THE CUP

Delicate, brightly colored raised flowers adorn the sides of this unusual footed Meissen teacup as well as the underside of the saucer. This example is perfect, but if a tiny flaw in the cup's glaze was detected at the factory in the early days of Meissen, a china decorator would have carefully painted a tiny insect over it. Customers eventually were so charmed by the bugs that they were later deliberately included on the cups and teapots.

SEPTEMBER

2019

Sunday	Monday	Tuesday	Wednesday	Thursday	Friday	Saturday
1	2 Labor Day	3	4	5	6	7
8 Grandparents Day	9	10	11	12	13	14
15	16	17	18	19	20	21 International Day of Peace
22	23 Queen's Birthday (WA Australia)	24	25	26	27	28
29 Rosh Hashanah begins at sundown	30					

"All well-regulated families set apart an hour every morning for tea and bread and butter."

—Joseph Addison, 1711

THE TEAPOT

TEA IN THE MORNING

There's nothing like an early morning "cuppa" to start off the day, especially when it's a hearty, full-bodied Assam poured from a teapot that prompts a smile. This clever *trompe l'oeil* earthenware teapot in the shape of an eggcup was crafted in the 1980s by the now-famous teapot designer Paul Cardew at his first studio, South West Ceramics in Devon, England. Today his firm, Cardew Design, is known worldwide for its imaginative pots. Attention to detail and a keen eye for the absurd are what make novelty pots memorable. The rakish "toast soldier" on the lid, the dripping egg yolk, and the perfectly reproduced faux silver spoon here are realized with skill and humor. Since this is morning tea, the real toast soldiers will soon be slathered with marmalade, which, according to teatime tradition, should be served at breakfast but never at afternoon tea.

THE TEA TABLE

TEA WITH LEMON

The custom of adding lemon to tea was very likely introduced to Europe by Queen Victoria. While visiting her eldest daughter, the consort of Prussian Emperor Frederick III, she was served tea in the Russian style, accompanied by jam, lumps of sugar, and lemon slices. Pleased with how the citrus brightened the flavor of black tea, the queen began offering lemon with tea. Other hostesses swiftly followed, and it was soon common practice for the tea table to include a plate of lemon slices.

OCTOBER

2019

Sunday	Monday	Tuesday	Wednesday	Thursday	Friday	Saturday
"The afternoon tea, or ceremonious at home, has for some years enjoyed a popularity that shows no signs of waning." —Emily Holt, *Encyclopaedia of Etiquette*, 1916		1	2	3	4	5
6	7 Labour Day (ACT, NSW & SA Australia) Queen's Birthday (QLD Australia)	8 Yom Kippur begins at sundown	9	10	11	12 Traditional Columbus Day
13	14 Columbus Day Observed Thanksgiving (Canada)	15	16	17	18	19
20	21	22	23	24	25	26
27	28 Labour Day (New Zealand)	29	30	31 Halloween		

THE TEAPOT

A GENTEEL LOW TEA

There is no respite more reviving than a tranquil hour (or more) spent sipping tea and nibbling diminutive refreshments in the company of close friends and compatible guests. In the mid-1800s, when afternoon tea first emerged as a fashionable ritual among the aristocracy, it was often referred to as "low tea." Most elegant homes and manor houses had at least one low table among the furnishings in the salon or withdrawing room. This low table became a convenient and logical spot on which to arrange the refreshments and tea set. An elegant tea equipage, such as this elaborately molded ca. 1898 Copeland late Spode fine bone china set, made in Stoke-on-Trent, England, would have been much admired by guests. The teapot is in a shape known as Louis XV. The sprightly pattern of the decoration, based on eighteenth-century Chinese porcelain designs, was printed, then hand-painted and gilded.

TEATIME TREATS

A STURDY HIGH TEA

Although the term "high tea" sounds fancier than "low tea," it actually refers to an informal, down-to-earth meal, also known as "meat" or "knife-and-fork" tea. Originating in the north of England during the Industrial Revolution, this working-class supper was served in modest homes at the end of the workday, around five or six o'clock. Strong tea, usually served in a sturdy mug, accompanied such hardy fare as cold ham, smoked fish, Welsh rarebit, or a piping-hot meat pie with vegetables. The meal ended with a plain cake.

TAPES
CHENILLE NEEDLES

NOVEMBER

2019

Sunday	Monday	Tuesday	Wednesday	Thursday	Friday	Saturday
"In faraway lands, or wherever you be, Friendship is welded by a good cup of tea." —MOTTO FROM A VINTAGE SAMPLER					1	2
3 U.S. Daylight Saving Time ends at 2:00 a.m.	4	5 Election Day	6	7	8	9 Mawlid an-Nabi begins at sundown
10	11 Veterans Day Remembrance Day (Canada)	12	13	14	15	16
17	18	19	20	21	22	23
24	25	26	27	28 Thanksgiving	29	30

THE TEAPOT

A SEWING CIRCLE TEA PARTY

A meeting of the sewing circle over tea was a gracious combination of two classic parlor pastimes. The star of this hospitable table is a rare "Roself" pattern Shelley earthenware teapot, ca. 1915, with a charming stenciled rose motif. The pattern was later made with orange roses and in a range of background colors. Shelley also made dainty china and Mabel Lucie Attwell's famed nursery wares. However, "Roself" was among its most dramatic designs. The unusual matte black background is reminiscent of Josiah Wedgwood's black basalt teapots of the 1770s. The dark color was much favored by vain hostesses who liked the way it showed off the whiteness of their hands as they poured tea.

TEAPOT HISTORY

THE SHELLEY GIRL

Shelley, one of the first potteries to hire a public relations firm, was unique among its peers in terms of marketing and publicity. There were Shelley doormats and color catalogs for shops, *Shelley Standard* magazine with sales tips and information, even a five-foot-high arching display stand for tea sets. And there was also the famous Shelley Girl, a stylish, foot-high china figurine displayed in shops between 1928 and 1937. She was posed with a teacup in one hand and a cookie in the other.

DECEMBER

2019

Sunday	Monday	Tuesday	Wednesday	Thursday	Friday	Saturday
1	2	3	4	5	6	7
8	9	10	11	12	13	14
15	16	17	18	19	20	21
22 Hanukkah begins at sundown	23	24	25 Christmas	26 Kwanzaa Boxing Day	27	28
29	30	31				

"Perhaps the best yuletide decoration is being wreathed in smiles."

—Anonymous

THE TEAPOT

A FESTIVE HOLIDAY TEA

The elaborate hospitality of the tea table took on a streamlined aspect following the 1925 Exposition des Arts Décoratifs et Industriels Modernes held in Paris. In contrast to the more ornate designs that prevailed during the Art Nouveau period, this exhibit, which inspired the Art Deco movement, introduced spare, clean lines inspired by sleek postwar industrial machines and ocean liners. The visual aesthetic was modern and understated. Metalsmiths in particular gravitated toward these ideas, and the bold simplicity of this Art Deco-inspired tea set by Bee & B. Powell epitomizes the genre. But however modern the teapot, teatime was still a traditional holiday festivity, and both family and guests could count on such classic seasonal goodies as miniature mince pies and tiny Christmas puddings. And there was goodwill in every cup of tea.

TEA ACCESSORIES

SILVER BELLS

The magical tinkling of the tea bell is a sign that something delicious is about to be served. The prettiest of these little tea-table amenities were produced in silver. Quite often their design matched the hostesses' silverware pattern, thus adding visual continuity to the table. The bells were generally used in one of two ways. For an informal tea, the mistress of the house might ring the bell to gather the family together. In more formal situations, when guests were visiting, she used the bell to summon household staff when it was teatime.

"Above all the refreshment of a good cup of tea!"

—Anna McNeill Whistler
(Whistler's Mother)

Celebrate a cherished ritual, a joyful midday interlude, a time for refreshment and conviviality. In a best-of collection from the Collectible Teapot & Tea calendar archives, a year of elegant teatime settings with gorgeous vintage teapots and dishes, sweet and savory nibbles, and vases brimming with bright, fresh flowers. Photographs are accompanied by charming tea-themed history, lore, and quotes.

JANUARY: *Winter splendor is reflected in a gilded James Sadler teapot.*

FEBRUARY: *An exquisite 1893 Royal Worcester tea set captures hearts.*

MARCH: *An elegant 1810 Ridgway porcelain pot holds plenty of tea for friends.*

APRIL: *Lovely Wedgwood Jasperware harmonizes with teatime in the conservatory.*

MAY: *Tidbits at a tea dance are served on Clarice Cliff "Bizarre" ware.*

JUNE: *The fresh beauty of this Royal Winton Chintz Ware will bloom forever.*

JULY: *Tea tastes best from a vividly colored 18th-century Nanking teapot.*

AUGUST: *Exquisite porcelain flowers bloom on an 1870 Meissen pot at a summertime tea.*

SEPTEMBER: *A whimsical South West Ceramics teapot holds early morning tea.*

OCTOBER: *A Louis XV–shape pot with a stunning floral pattern adds a touch of elegance to any afternoon tea.*

NOVEMBER: *Decoratively stenciled roses bloom on a rare Shelly "Roself" teapot.*

DECEMBER: *The delights of a silver Art Deco tea set light up the holiday table.*

Workman Publishing Co., Inc.
New York, NY 10014 • pageaday.com

workman

$14.99 U.S.
$19.99 Can.
$25.00 Aus.
Printed in South Korea

ISBN 978-1-5235-0315-5